Through the Canopy

Linda Breeden

Through the Canopy

Copyright © 2012 Linda Breeden

Cover picture Copyright © 2012 Linda Breeden
Little Wing Publications
Safety Harbor, Florida 34695

All rights reserved.

ISBN-13: 978-0615700441

Linda Breeden

For my family

Special thanks to

Ron, who taught me to see "through the canopy"

Jim, for being my sounding board, willing devil's advocate and constant source of inspiration through my many rewrites.

Fellow PINAWOR writers for your many suggestions and critiques.

Through the Canopy

Contents:

Letter to an ex	pg 3
For you	pg 6
Exiled	pg 8
The shore	pg 9
Alien	pg 10
Green eyes	pg 12
Love's unfolding	pg 14
Harlequin	pg 15
Canyon song	pg 17
The window	pg 18
From Jersey	pg 21
Quiet voice	pg 22
Past life	pg 23
Arcslycus	pg 25
Firefly	pg 27
Homogenized road trip	pg 29
Fishing for love	pg 31
Sympathy for the devil	pg 33
The ogre	pg 35
Read me a poem	pg 37
Missing	pg 38
Say it with flowers	pg 39
Undercurrent	pg 41
Savannah	pg 42
Escape	pg 44

Linda Breeden

Song of war	pg 45
Tree	pg 47
Cataract moon	pg 49
The shifting season of Rachel	pg 51
Katrina	pg 53
Beginnings	pg 55
Meuse Argonne	pg 56
Instructions	pg 57
The ambush	pg 59
Fallen son	pg 62
Symbiosis	pg 64
Writing at the beach	pg 66
Caterpillar spring	pg 68
The front porch swing	pg 71
Nurse	pg 72
The barn	pg 73
The white bones of winter	pg 75
Spirit	pg 77
Sleep walker	pg 79
Because	pg 82
Joy	pg 83
La Giaconda	pg 85
Outlanders	pg 86
Pied piper	pg 87
Atlantis	pg 88
Majillon	pg 90

Through the canopy

Linda Breeden

Forward

This book is a journey, a poetic journey strung loosely together by threads of possibility. Many of these poems explore the idea that we may have existed before, some celebrate and examine life and humanity through ordinary or dramatic events.

In the lives of most men and women there are, from time to time, places or people they come upon which have an unexpected familiarity. Most likely brushed aside as fancied, still these moments spark the imagination and fuel the fires of human yearning for something beyond the incumbent explanations of life and death.

Whether or not you choose to consider this, I hope you will enjoy the poems.

Through the canopy

Through the canopy of a single lifetime, memories filter like sunlight through the leaves, seeking every rift and fissure in the insularity of our one-life conviction, reminding and persuading us that we always were, and will forever be.

Linda Breeden

In every lifetime there is Love...

Letter to an ex.

The sun slips low in the darkening sky as I gather these thoughts, so many years gone,
relics of you and me, strewn along yesterday's path,
like breadcrumbs awaiting memory's silent footfall.

I follow their trail and wonder why,
as night wakes from its diurnal slumber,
I need to reach you, to tell you who I have become and where life has taken me since it last took me from you.

As I return, fading from present like dusk's umbral face, I hear the old chime clock in the hall, a constant sentinel of the hours which slip so slyly by as I risk again the joy and the pain I have not felt for so long.

An eclipse of dreams, our goodbye left all that remained a barren 'scape of squandered love,
but with that parting came resolve to seek a larger world, to fly from that lonely place into the arms of providence.

Panaji, Jaipur, Udaipur, worlds away, where beauty and need formed such sharp contrast that my soul bled from its edge.
Here, a man who would follow the path you forged in my heart, a man whose insight and generous spirit were an intimate home that found me so far from mine.

In the years that followed, across India,
the impoverished places of Earth, we travelled

Linda Breeden

hunger's divergent landscapes, searching for voice to quell the inequities harbored everywhere behind the hollow eyes of children.

Through it all I wrote, attempting to frame the world's inhumanity with words inadequate to the task ... and he would listen, like you once had, as they flowed from me - a stream swollen by a torrent of human tears.

It was in Cambodia's spring, before monsoons swept up from the south and all life fell beneath the hypnotic din of the ceaseless rain, that I lost him. Beneath a moonlit sky, cobalt blue and flecked with the gaze of distant worlds, he fell along the road, a wayfarer 'cross the threshold to forever.

And so too I died, to be reborn again in the voices that coursed around and through me,
in the lives that coaxed me from my days of impoverished thought and the debilities of sorrow... for we are a storied race, rich with divergent dreams and journeys that must be imparted.

And so I wrote...

In days between, when the journey found me undecided where to travel, I thought of him, and of you, and the story that connects our lives.

...

There is comfort in the familiar trappings of this room, the roll-top desk with its dark patina of pensive days, the soft glow of the hurricane lamp, a gentle insight into night, like the stars appearing now

Through the canopy

through the oriel, ushered by the quiet clack of keys.

I hope you will realize it's not unhappiness
that shares my bed, or emptiness that attends me in
the reflective hours of the day, for life has been worth
the losses and hope remains untarnished by
compromise.

Still, there is no one here to gather my convictions to
their heart or listen when reason and self assurance
fail to comfort me...

Perhaps that is why I write you now...
not to rekindle any long extinguished flame or
sow seeds of regret in an infertile land.

No, I realize now, it is just to feel that connection,
to touch again a familiar heart, and though I may never
send this, to write once more with words of love to
someone who once loved me.

Linda Breeden

For you

I remember the one with the wry smile and the sea in
his eyes, with a penchant for long-suffering women of
noble breeding...

For him I endured the hardships of fictive
misfortune, crafting my sorrow and my bearing so
well that even I believed.

And the one with wanderlust in his heart,
unfettered by material concerns,
who loved freedom more than the choke of luxury
or the confines of expectancy...

For him I relinquished the trappings of a lavish life,
rejoicing in paucity and privation
and a spirit expunged of need.

And would I forget the artist, his passion forged in
the same hell-fire kiln as his bronze, loving hands
fashioning clay to life, in the breaking light of
inspiration?...

For him I cultivated awe, born of the sweet suasive
virtue of his dream, my thoughts soon disdaining
mediocrity and the mean strivings of commonality.

But you...

you alone my love, will I remember, most real,
most true. When this life narrows to its close and
memories have become my spirit's provender,

Through the canopy

sustaining and renewing my days,

In the gentle rush of recall, you'll return like the lap of
the sea, a cogent declaration of my soul's own worth,
delivered soft as the hush of wonder,
always back, always back to me.

Linda Breeden

Exiled

You turn away, penitent.
Your smile, a thin goodbye,
leaves me desperate,
a low flyer over jutting cliffs,
praying for mercy and the
winged salvation of the wind's lift.

I watch your stride
recede from view,
the parallel lines of our lives
collapsed to a single stroke,
a razor's path,
a point, to soon
disappear from sight.

In the shadow of your wake,
no solace waits,
no compass for this exiled angel
to find her way home ...

to light,

to love,

to self.

The shore

Does the shore gladden when waves retreat, pull back their watery mantle, to reveal the sun and sky?
Does it delight the chance now to become the surface, to reflect the light, to define the contour of the land?

Or, does it mourn the touch withdrawn,
the watery embrace recanted,
in whose aqueous arms it once lay a silent and sated lover?

You dip your quill in love;
your thoughts imbued with promise.
Words flow from your hand,
wash over me, then retreat softly .
I glimpse the sun and the breathy sky
but long to hold your words forever on my shore.

Through the Canopy

Alien

When you don't see...

I watch your eyes,
the azure net of your gaze
thrown across a blue expanse,
pulling it to you,
scanning that unreachable divide
between sea and sky and
hungering for a thing unspoken,

and I know,
you've been too long here...

like a seafarer resigned to shore,
whose blood rises in moon-pulled tide, and
lips taste of brine,
whose spirit longs for the uncertainty of days
spent on a trackless, shifting world,
wooing that capricious lover,
searching always further,
beyond the horizon,
beyond tomorrow,
always beyond.

But should you
linger long with me...

tethered to my days by unseen chains,
our contentment warm and easy as a windless night,
I will pray you home, but curse the ragged winds of
change that someday will blow you there,

Through the canopy

gone, beyond the camber of the earth,
no longer an interloper in this world,
yearning for flight ...

and the distant voice of home.

Linda Breeden

Green eyes

In your green eyes, that vale in spring,
whose verdant slopes brushed the sky,
where once I walked midst perfumed blooms,
heady-scented on the breeze, lost in dreams of youth.

And in those eyes as pale as jade,
that long-lost city 'neath the sea;
Atlantis shone her wizard halls,
lofty, carved of Earth's fair flesh
and magic filled my soul.

You my love, with beryl gaze,
such gentle pools of knowing light,
looked on me and quenched my need,
parched from sorrow's cruel drought
and offered hope's sweet vow.

All my joys and all my dreams
reflected there in your sweet gaze,
a window in that darkest tower,
my heart so long imprisoned there,
did take to wing and soar.

But now my love our paths must part
and you need honor duty's vow,
this fragile span of time we shared,
a chapter closed and bound by love,
preserved in fate's embrace.

But somewhere, in our unborn days,
when future dreams and memories wed,

Through the canopy

when dreary charge has set you free
I know I'll find myself again
In your loving green eyes.

Linda Breeden

Love's unfolding

You came to me where contentment had staked its
claim. Territorial, abiding no feral thoughts of longing,
it cleared the underbrush of passion and abandon
and the reedy trunks of hope that sprung in my heart.

Life was ordered and I, cloistered far
from storms of desire and hungering,
heeded the advice of complacent angels,
couching every thought of yearning as frivolous or
vain.

So long I dwelt there, faithful to routine and solitude,
the sameness so loud, I never heard the nascent
sirens of change calling me to flight nor glimpsed your
eyes shining into every measured moment of my days.

Until, wondrous, you arrived,
sprung from universes of light and meaning,
drawn complete through the sorrow and sinew of
evanescent worlds dying on distant plains in
forgotten time.

Here at last, awakening my heart from slumber,
with the chaos of your touch,
the order of my days wheeling away
like galaxies let loose their stations.

Lover, what divine anarchy you bring
from contentment's demise
and love's unfolding.

Harlequin

Why are you here, Love?
Why pretend, after so long,
such spurious affection for this heart, alone in love?

Have you seceded this endless span
to affect a hero's return,
and I, the fool in harlequin, still await?

Do you relish my unrequited desire,
a sadist devouring a masochist's pain?
Your blade sharp but your caress so tender,
I don't mind the blood spill from my side.

Am I a discarded pursuit,
a dirty secret never to be mentioned in polite
company; your touch here to declare our alliance
and so secure my oath to confidence?

If you do not want me, why beguile?
Do you fear a future where loneliness
will press you to flight and, my love,
the unguarded road, your path away?

Lust is a poor imposter but so very persuasive.
Had it not seized love's voice,
espousing assurances of forever,
its strained chords would have betrayed you.

But you are the great ventriloquist,
the remorseless paramour,
deceiving not only your intimates but love itself.

Linda Breeden

And I, the fool,
hoarding pictures of our days,
like a jester's counterfeit coins,
hope still to spend them in receipt of a life with you.

Canyon song

Again we meet, so I'll tell you this;
it is the music of the canyon come back to my soul.

Along paths of worn rock, smoothed slick
by the centuries' dry longing, its melody
flows like the spill of night into the hollow cup of day.

Beyond your form, welcome in my need
as sunlight that plumbs the dark crevasse,
you carry the song of light upon your lips and
the thunder's trailing rumble in your eyes.

In the inhale and exhale of your nearness,
I breathe the aspen and the pinion as they sway
in rhythmic lauding to the urging of the wind.

You are the high arch of sky that calls me now.
Risen from sheer cliffs and ravines of jagged hunger,
I rejoice in your eternal song,
a tone poem to give my spirit voice.

Linda Breeden

The window

Look at me,
since you've gone,
the thought of you, so loud,
I can hardly hear.

How is it you speak to me
more clearly in your absence,
than in all the days we shared our smiles?

Why do I trace the lines of your face
and see the passion in your eyes,
long after your spark has grown cold,
through eyes that only now can see?

I scarce believe the way I feel:
alone, after what we should have felt,
I wonder where the torrent, the raging river of desire?
For only dried bottomland lies before me,
that river's trace, scorched by disappointment's
burning glare.

Why, in this unsuspecting moment,
though I argued harshly, I'd never care,
has this window opened in my heart
to admit the interloper, love?

Why now,
when your heart has closed that fissure,
braced strong against winds of longing,
a fortress stayed from within?

Through the canopy

Look at me,
I sit on the banks of this barren riverbed
and pray for rain.
In the shadow of your keep
my heart has flown my breast,
and this love for you cannot be quieted.

Linda Breeden

In every lifetime there is remembrance...

From Jersey...

From Jersey, my memory rises now like the steam off the hood of our old Pontiac as it struggled to throw off winter's frosty embrace.

Clattering out of the warmth, metal lunch pail clutched close, I'd plie' across the icy sidewalk to the driveway, making deals with gravity

and yank the wagon's door, its lock exerting a frozen stubbornness, to finally fling myself on the seat, out of reach of the bully wind.

Always the same routine, my small body drawn up like a downhill racer, I'd plead through chattering teeth, "turn up the heat," and eye the dashboard.

Nose and face flushed pink, breath escaping in humid clouds to fog the windows,
I'd fumble with numb fingers to stretch my mini-skirt to my knees.
...
So many years since, my days now spent in more temperate climes, I can feel those chilly, childhood memories return.

Like a smile they make me warm.

Linda Breeden

Quiet voice

That Winter of '59
snow fell on our town like a downy baptism,
a hushed urgency weeping its white dismay onto
every fragile twig and waking shoot that dared rise
before the spring.
So heavy and wet it lay that branches snapped and
lines sagged, finally giving way to burden…

'til all that remained was stillness.

Gone the crackling rush of electrons, the flicker of
lights, the magnetic hum of modernity that rung from
every home…

absorbed in the muffled drifts which swallowed all but
the "white noise" of the snow's falling and the laconic
peeping of the chickadees and titmice.

In our farmhouse, no TV, no radio, no illumination,
save the light of candles and companionship,
of neighbors who'd journeyed backyards
to offer their thawed sacrifices upon the altar of our
old gas stove.
…
My thoughts sometimes struggle to regain those
days, obscured now by the press of age, yet,
when the first crystal herald of memory falls
I seek the long-gone silence of that world,
listening past the chaos of the day
to hear again Earth's quiet voice.

Past life

I was an architect then.
Strange to still recall that time
when memory has elected a much closer periphery.

Those were the roaring years
and we, the prime movers of that new world,
drew forth the life of the city from parchment DNA
and double dimensions.

No mere mortals we,
but art deco demigods
erecting monuments to our own providence

With quixotic regard
we watched the behemoths eruct from the earth,
our great granite offspring 'come an empire of stone.

Angular beauties thrusting upward,
steel arms stretched to touch the sky,
geometric sirens tempting the heavens to earth.

And from the speakeasies and the dancehalls,
the melodies rife with rhythm spilled into the streets
like syncopated prayers to the gods of gaiety.

You on my arm, we walked the night among them -
two sojourners chasing a ribbon of stars -
beneath our feet a galaxy in concrete.

The big war had passed, the other not yet begun.
What but death itself could challenge us,

Linda Breeden

or quell the city's nascent spirit?

But pass we did,
slip from the hand of fortune,
and the kingdom we had shaped from our own ambitions.

Strange, now, to recall that time,
this flat prairie plain stretched forever before me,
you no longer by my side.

But I remember what it was like to be a god,
to sculpt a world from just an idea

I remember. I remember it still — I always will.

Arcslycus

For ten thousand lifetimes we toiled,
slaves of Arcslycus, drudging through our days,
cogs in the machine, hammering, polishing
welding, glazing that splendid floating city on
eternity's rim.

With no more thought than the tools in our hands,
we executed our tasks, never counting the hours or
the years as they crept so slowly by,
as flesh sagged beneath time's burden and
wore thin with the repetition of our duties.

Our bodies, held in pawn, from life to death to
life again we perished and were formed in new flesh,
living souls, refitted like machines, erecting great
tabernacles of glass and stone to worship the
rapacious gods of grandeur.

No top or bottom, no up or down, an Escher
drawing going nowhere 'cross an endless void of
space, that city's vast extent, rising and falling then
arching away in great heaves of polished stone,
cobbled so deftly together by the hands of captive
beings.

Monolithic slabs like stratus shale, floating sleek and
glistening, their cascading stairs like falling water,
twisted and curved through the vastness of space,
where sometimes we'd gaze at the thrusting spirals,
ripping the fabric of the sky, as they pointed us from
bondage.

Linda Breeden

I don't remember who first had the thought, whether
taskmaster or slave, the first musing of that virgin idea,
that would signal Arcslycus' doom, but it spread
'cross that realm like a deadly whisper and
soon each began to wonder.

For no one had asked, or ever questioned,
how that massive city could float.
No, none had considered it was simply thought,
collective agreement that formed its framework – the
mortar that held the brick, the steel that strung the
web.

So, of course, what felled Arcslycus, and crumbled
that glorious realm, was not the thought that slaves
should be free or that masters should have a
conscience, or even that governance should be
overthrown.
It was simply the idea of gravity.

Firefly

Where have you been my little one?
Look at you – here but still not back.

I remember you,
seems like yesterday, or has it been years
since they said your smile too bright,
your laughing eyes and tinkling voice -- a dissonance
in their new order of prescribed and proper behavior.

I remember you.
You greeted me with a face like the sky, and
small arms overflowing with wishes
like fresh cut sheaves of wheat.
You drew your dreams on the sidewalk and
we played hopscotch from painter to poet to
astronaut as you beamed a crooked moon from your
sky.

What did they do to you when they gave you those
pills, said you were too "alive," too active
to be normal

or tolerated......?

I remember you.
You were never normal.
You were a firefly hovering over a field of Earth-
bound crawlers, above the rest, delighting in the
freedom of your flight.

Linda Breeden

In every lifetime there is laughter...

Homogenized road trip

"I really needed this," you repeat once more,
"a change, a little variety, a break from the everyday."

I take your hand, as outside, nature rushes past.

Here the trees are not the same.
they bend to a brusquer wind,
their bare branches pink as a debutante's blush
as they wait the cold coming-out of spring.

But the highway remains unchanged,
the long stretch of pavement, striped up the middle
like the perfect stitch-line of grandma's Singer.
Triangular commentary and rectangular
pronouncements tell us "where to get off."

Between towns topography reinvents itself as
shrugged shoulders and endless crowding pines curve
away to yawning gullies and fields of harrowed hay.

It's like a painting, you exclaim, but soon neon orange
letters loom into view, commanding our attention and
informing us that we'll shortly be approaching
Big Bob's Western Outfitters, the next "must see"
pit-stop on our journey through small town americana.

"Need a new pair of boots?" you ask, your sense of
"consumer obligation" showing.

"No, but I could use a bite to eat.
How about some lunch?" I reply,

Linda Breeden

as we return our gaze to the windows and beyond.

Cracker Barrel, Wendy's, Waffle House and
Hardees, BP, Citgo, Chevron and Subway,
the same signs we've seen across three borders,
like aluminum giraffes craning their necks
above the buildings to vie for our attention.

"Sure. Cracker Barrel again?" you offer
unabashedly, as a few disoriented flakes dodge our
car and swirl away toward the road.

"Cracker Barrel it is," I say, "but next time let's try
something different.
Let's try Waffle House."

Fishing for love

It was her fuck-all attitude had done it!
She was a clever one, that,
with her holier-than-thou demeanor
and her holes-in-the-pockets threads.

Not one of those "Stepford" wives,
he'd become so accustomed to -
coy flirtations and emotional itineraries,
all neatly packaged with impeccable taste, in Armani.

No, she was a girl who'd slice off your ear,
then scold for blood on the rug ,
the perfect foil to insincere proposals
the perfect dare to conceit.

When he cast the bait, with confident flair,
she tugged and threw it back on board,
making him wonder if he fished the wrong pond,
but signaling start of the game.

He was a handsome lothario,
quite charming, as most had assumed.
She was a fiery raven-haired beauty,
very used to getting her way.

He with his frat-boy background
and lexicon of smarmy white lies,
oiling his way 'cross the fertile landscape
of ample and willing women,

She with insouciant candor,

Linda Breeden

so easily fierce when chafed,
with all the tolerance of a taunted badger
and a streak as stubborn as taffy.

So they began the eternal dance,
each to a different rhythm -
ballroom and hip-hop, salsa and bee-bop –
each out of step with the other.

Their passion was feral and savage,
their warfare the stuff of legend.
They couldn't be friends, they couldn't part,
the best they could do was to marry.

Sympathy for the Devil

He waited on the floor, motionless.
after the screaming stopped – my screaming, that is,
I looked a little closer at what I surmised was stark terror.
He was frozen, as were we both,
two life forms transfixed by each other's presence,
playing chicken on the kitchen floor.

I watched his antennae rotate, feeling the air for
clues. My breathing was halting and shallow.
I could almost read his thoughts, would this be his
last moment on earth before oblivion?"
I surmised he could read mine.

Then it happened, just as I raised the rolled-up
newspaper to strike the fatal blow.
I'd never have imagined it, but I began to soften,
looking at him there on the floor, his little brown body
frozen with fear, his six legs quivering as he braced
himself for the worst.

I swore he was reasoning with me telepathically,
pleading his case for clemency – poor little thing.
What had he really done to deserve my wrath?
Just because he'd strayed wrongly into my home,
didn't I walk outdoors in his domain?
Where was the harm in his losing his way in mine?

Then the screen door slammed and you called as you
entered. I turned. He ran, and in that brief second my
sympathy evaporated like a bottle of *Everclear* on a

Linda Breeden

summer's day.

I screamed once more and you sprung to my side like an action hero, and with a steel-toed size 13, you crushed him flat.

The ogre

I ran into an ogre the other day.
He was standing in the unemployment line down at the county building, shifting slowly from side to side like a great fleshy pendulum.
He looked at me with those brooding black eyes of his, as if to say "there are no more fairy tales."

Still, I had to work up the courage to speak to him. Seems the Brothers Grimm hadn't embellished his attributes, with that thundercloud brow, those great stalagmite tusks jutting from his lower jaw
and a copse of matted hair providing refuge for a sprawling community of vermin.

"Tough times," I commented in his general direction, unsure of his proficiency with words. To my surprise, he answered back in perfect linguistic form with a voice, rough, I imagined, from too much fe-fi-foing, yet still polished and very properly British.

"Seems there's just not room for my kind any more," he sighed, a tear escaping his eye. "The castles back home have all cut back, economic problems, you know. They asked me to leave – one less mouth to feed. I guess I shouldn't have eaten the Duke's cat."

Before I could ask him the question there on my tongue, "Next," came over the speaker, and the gloomy giant sidled to the counter of a panicked clerk, pushing forms through the narrow window, making sure none of his fingers lingered.

Linda Breeden

I wanted to speak to him some more
but he was gone by the time I'd finished and though I
tried very hard to find him, searching the men's room
and the parking lot for clues, no trace remained of
that down-and-out Ogre, and I wondered about his
fate.

So, if you see him, please inquire as to his condition,
All in all, I'm sure he's not a bad guy, no different than
the rest of us in this less than fairy-tale situation,
wrestling with tough economic times. Ask him over for
a cup of coffee, I'm sure he'd appreciate the gesture,
......that is, if you don't have cats.

Read me a poem

Read me a simple poem,
one I needn't work to understand,
a poem in primary colors:
apple red, sky blue and sun yellow.

Recite some lithe and carefree verse -
short words galloping 'cross the page.
I need no long plodding rhymes
that want to run back to the barn before they're read.

Read me a poem without thees and thous
and no subjunctive mood please.
Construct it simply like linguistic Legos -
the younger version for 3-5 years.

I want a poem like my first grade teacher -
one to wrap my knuckles and say, "listen up!"
I won't chase the meaning under the desk
nor muse from a stool in the corner.

I'd like an easy poem from basic shapes-
circles and triangles and squares.
Don't read me a page from advanced geometry;
I don't want to nap right now.

Tell me a poem that won't strain my wit
nor leave me panting and spent,
something straightforward and undemanding,
'cause it's been a very long day!

Linda Breeden

Missing

You didn't come home last night;
left me fending off those gnawing worries.

Were you lying in a ditch,
abducted, strolling the quarry road or,
though I hate to admit it would be worse,
had you found comfort in another's arms,
a more welcoming table,
a softer bed, a fireside embrace?

But here you are this morning at the door,
hungry and full of meows to
scold this contrite doorkeeper.

Say it with flowers,

They were an affirmation in a no-frills carafe,
an assortment of stems and promises,
his commitment newly proffered in an
array of pinks and reds.

She welcomed them at her door,
gathering them in like kittens from the stoop,
embracing their glorious blooms
and the implication of their coming.

His truer heart now shone
in a claret hue of roses, as lavender
spires of liatris vied with mums and
carnations, for attention of her eye.

On mercurial feet they'd winged their way to her,
petalled seraphim offering his contrition,
love's eternal emissaries clothed in nature's splendor,
fresh as the crocus' rising.

She arranged them precisely in prominence, in
the entry to showcase their beauty, as
she read the card he'd enclosed for her heart...

"Have a nice life, I've moved to Zimbabwe."

Linda Breeden

In every lifetime there is conflict and prayers for peace...

Undercurrent

Beneath the table's surface,
swirling round the legs of the Chippendale chairs,
there's a current sliding past our knees and whirling
invisible eddies as it wends its way through the room.

You fiddle with your glass, launching a forced smile
downstream on the unseen tide.
I glimpse the frosty draft flicker the candle flame.
Our thoughts fall unspoken on the widening shore.

Moments gasp and flounder in the undertow as
questions rise within me...

What hidden deed slips here secreted from the light
of day, eroding the underpinning of my faith and
washing promises upon the jagged rocks of suspicion
like so much sea wrack?

Maybe you think I'll never know.

Perhaps I never will.

There's a current sliding past our knees tonight,
winding dark beneath the seemly conversation,
rising swiftly on a crest of doubt,
to sweep my trust to sea.

Linda Breeden

Savannah....

Let's go swing on the front porch swing,
back to a simpler time.
We'll have some tea and biscuits
and some of my blackberry jam.

Let's profess we don't have a care –
that this land of ours is not cleaved.
We'll swing and listen to cricket songs,
and the tree frogs chirp like rain.

Let's go savor this guileless time
of grace and sweet belonging
in the jasmine air of this sultry night
we'll count the magnolia stars.

Let's pretend the war's not nigh
and all we love not in peril.
The hoot-owl still calls from the cypress hollow,
the bullfrog croaks in the swamp

Let's float our prayers on the sighing breeze
that the yanks won't find their way here,
that our rebs still struggle to free the south
and our sons don't lie dying.

.....

Let's not shed a tear for fair Savannah,
on this last of these innocent nights,
though loud the rumble of distant cannon
and the silence of God in my thoughts.

Through the canopy

Let's go swing on the front porch swing,
back to a simpler time.
We'll have some tea and biscuits
and some of my blackberry jam

Linda Breeden

Escape

Four a.m. on the highway,
darkness seduces my mind,
the lonely lure of untraveled roads,
the thrill of stealthy escape.

My flight away in a ship of steel,
headlights augur the way
through the murk of morn,
the pain of your words,
still sharp as the lambent stars.

Stretched before me this gunmetal ribbon
rises and twists like a curl of smoke.
White striped, glinting to gloom, it urges
me ever onward.

From the void the radio keeps time to staccato
reflectors pulsing their rhythms,
Monk and Coltrain - jazz in the dark,
how I wish we could have been saved.

Song of war

Last night I woke from startled sleep -
I dreamed that you had fallen, at the
hands of a foe, 'neath Thrace's soil,
never to return to me.

Last night I gazed on starlit sea and
called your name out low.
I watched your sails off Scotland's shore
billow your goodbye.

Last night I watched through tearful eyes
my brave brought home from war,
no longer fleet, no longer strong,
your face to smile no more.

I'll be back my love when the war is done,
when right has conquered wrong,
I'll come sailing home from vanquished lands
and we will be as one.

Last night I dreamt our life, long past,
if I had only known,
in the chilling air of that Aleutian dawn,
you'd offer your last embrace.

Last night I saw through time's thin veil
the promise you had made,
through all this thorny course of time
your love for me remained.

Last night I held you in my arms

Linda Breeden

and felt the soul of you.
I realized you'd come back to me
and all my dreams were true.

I'll be back my love when the war is done,
when right has conquered wrong
I'll come sailing home from vanquished lands
and we will be as one.

Through the canopy

Tree....

You subscribe to no politics, no philosophy or creed.
Never a radical fomenting the masses,
nor operative in secret cabal,
deposing the current regime.

Tree...

No slick hustler you, whispering shady promises
to gullible clientele or huckstering elixirs of syrupy
salvation to naive optimists

In boardrooms of multinationals
you'll not be found guilty of illicit trading
or denounced for ethics lapses
with the futures of your dependants.

Tree...

In your darkest hour we'll not find you, a jingoist,
ready finger poised on the button,
to make righteous argument
with the burned-out throats of your enemies,

nor leading pogroms
in the lands of your fathers,
the standard of hate lofted overhead
as the soul of that nation bleeds.

Tree.....

What must you think of this world before you,

Linda Breeden

so unsatisfied, each, with their place?
Do you have a viewpoint, can you feel any sorrow
for this dark and mislaid human race?

Cataract moon

Weary night, your watchful moon, a cataract eye,
casts its filmy gaze on the Earth below.
And wary it watches, chary of her heart her motives
and her pleas, ever silent, ever patient in the
darkness.

What monstrous arms has it beheld
roil the cauldrons of human passion and
churn her centuries with despair and want?
What hope, its light, to comfort her children,
the lambs of man slaughtered on altars of greed?

Night gather your voice for your eye has clouded
with ancient tears long since spent, and
cry to the Godhead, pray wake from your sleeping
and deliver this earth to peace.

Linda Breeden

In every lifetime there is loss...

The shifting season of Rachel

The day weeps.
Crystalline tears flood their unseen swales and
rush to fill the space between us.

Aqueous fingers yearn for the comfort of
another's touch, kindred souls,
folded close by the commonality of loss,
so singular yet so plural in its sway.

Humanity's breath draws deep, the
lodestone of our affection absent from the path
home.

Certain you will not return, we grieve,
unwrapping pictures of your days like
fine china packed away behind our eyes.

You turn on pointed toes,
arabesque smiles proffered to willing lookers,
auburn strands on magnolia-petal skin,

With outstretched arms you welcome us all, the
reticent, the recalcitrant, those lost and those found,
welcome us with guileless decorum
into the vestibule of your heart.

In the hollow between the moments
compassion echoes its quiet chords to
comfort friends left empty by your loss,
and the day testifies of love.

Linda Breeden

You speak, voiceless, and with silent intent
death is qualified, no longer goodbye,
only a shifting season before we shall see you again.

Through the canopy

Katrina...

New Orleans, I dream your death.
In darkness, a thousand, thousand voices cry out.
With incorporeal regard I listen as beneath a pall of
fetid water, endless questions eruct from your bowels:
where is help, where is comfort, where is God?

Still my tears do not wake me.

In the turbid hours before the dawn a mother weeps.
I watch her clutch a lifeless child to her heart
and draw a long wail, as if to exhale her grief into a
world too small to contain it.

Still my tears do not wake me.

The forsaken and the sick, everywhere
lie dying beneath the folds of my lids,
their voices muffled by pleas of husbands, wives,
lovers and children to a God no longer there.
And from my sleep I cry aloud, open your eyes,
open your eyes and set them free.

Still my tears do not wake me.

In the distance the crack of gunfire
speaks to a world gone mad
as angry men, unable now to help,
seek only destruction to be cause.

As a sick body turns upon itself
the depraved, soothed only by the balm of hate,

Linda Breeden

heed the siren song of wickedness
and raise their hands to each other
in the opaque recesses of the day.

Still my tears do not wake me.

On the rooftops your people thirst and breathe the
acrid air of fear.
Your raucous voice, heard so soon ago lies hushed
and still.
The wail of trombones from your honky-tonks,
is now but lingering memory of a carnival faith,
shared by all who harbored within your walls.

City of sorrow, hold me to your breast.
Let me still feel your heartbeat,
pale and shallow as your breath,
laboring in the dank and rotting air.
Tell me that someday, my tears will wake me
and I will once again look to find you whole.

Beginnings

If all beginnings and endings are just junctures
on the same forever road and the moon but a floater
across the dark eye of night, appearing then not, as it
follows the ancient groove of the sky,

so life insists from its fragile germ upon continuance,
radiating outward in conquest of oblivion,
to embrace all things conceivable.

You tell me that you are leaving,
another rotation 'round the Sun, this time alone.
What beginning will our ending bring,
what new path to follow?

I smell the jasmine on the night breeze.
Andalusia, beneath the terracotta quilt of your
huddled roofs, the steps of Malaga call my feet to
the sea.

Linda Breeden

Meuse-Argonne

The years have fled my life,
still I tarry on this foreign field.
Above my grave a welt of white crosses rises somber
and silent to wheel away in flawless curve across the
viridian plain.

I am stitched to this place in time, their sharp needles
of glory have bound me to the past, the symmetry of
death, its manicured grounds and marble monuments,
a stark contrast to the chaos and imperfection of life.

For decades they've come, the children, the loved
ones, the friends, come to find their past, mourn their
dead, place their hands upon the pulse of history,
thrumming its strained cadence from deep within the
belly of the earth.

There is a gravity to this place that pulls the living to
it, a current in their blood that seeks the farthest
shores of human endeavor. Caught in eddies of time
they are drawn by their own unremembered days of
oblivion.

Beyond these arbor walls, the land rolls away to
tomorrow holding its sorrows close to its breast,
whispering no remembrances of Argonne, or the
blood spilled into eternity, to flow forever down the
river Meuse.

Instructions

My thoughts hold me here,
at least a little while longer,
like loose threads catching a splintered rail
as I try to hurry out this door.

So, I'll relate what I can
of those that lie spread around me, though time is
short and so many have already been packed away
for my long journey ahead.

Engage your daughter.
She'll be a young woman soon,
needing to shoulder the weight of an absent mother,
with a still-small child.

Use her and love her.
She's smart and already knows much.
Let her do the laundry.
She knows to separate the whites and the colors,
when I'm sure you wouldn't think twice to do so.

Two or three times a year
put a cup of bleach in the ac line.
The step-ladder's in the hall closet
— watch the second rung,
the funnel's under the sink.

Soon the freezer will need defrosting.
I'm sorry I didn't have time.
Eat things from earliest to latest.
I've marked dates on all the wrappers.

Linda Breeden

There are two turtle doves nesting in the gable by
Lily's room.
She loves them, even with their feathers and their
pooping. I'm sure that's all I need to tell you.

And Sydney, our woman child,
needs to be reminded to go to scouts - sometimes she
won't want to, though she's always happy when she
returns, exclaiming to me the fine time she's had.

Last week I noticed that dead tree in the back yard,
the one with all the neighborhood kids' names carved
in it, looks like a swarm of honey bees have taken up
residency. Too bad we don't have a bear.

So many things to clutter the mind.
I guess that's what keeps life moving forward -
the maintaining of ordinary things
balanced with dreams of what could be.

But now those things slip away
and another life calls me forward -
always through fear's door,
the dream of what could be.

In the ordinary things
you'll find comfort.
In our children's eyes you'll find love.
And in tomorrow, you may again find me.

The ambush

Without premonition or portent, you are here,
sucked from the mire of stagnant hope through a
wormhole in time, to ambush my world.
And from the repercussions of your words, and
the sight of you here, I know Earth must surely
have shifted on its axis.

I love you still...

Four little words - forty years gone,
that incautious remark spilling out of your
mouth like so much miscalculated
whipped cream atop the pie.
You, two wives and no children later,
me with a daughter and a long-dead husband
still roaming the halls of my thoughts,
and between us no word, save the idle gossip
of third rate friends.

I love you still...

Those words, you here, flashes of lightening
sundering my world, smothering my emotions
like settling ash, their fallout burning my senses to a
charred landscape, a desolate plain of our almost life.

Our dream, its seed, still cradled in the bosom of
sorrow, took root there in the fertile loam of love's
yearning.
Never a feral thought of dissent, we stitched our lives
together with devotion's sturdy thread and wrapped

Linda Breeden

the broad swath of tomorrow 'round our shoulders,

until the ruin in Vietnam called you, and the conspiracy of time and duty cleaved our world into soldier and sadness.

    For so many years
    No word came...

Married when you returned, overcome to see your name finally expunged from the list of the missing, I tried to find you. But time had swallowed your trace and the demands of responsibility disallowed a continued quest.

How could I have known, my search in vain, for so many years your only view, the landscape of despair from your hospital window?
Manhood and mind in the purgatory of the broken, your legs sacrificed for the aegis of gaunt democracy in jungles of perdition.

    I didn't know...

A comfort then to not, to think you safe and whole, that you had survived Hell, and I your loss.
Hoping in my imaginings, you thought of me and reflected gently on the sweet analogy of souls we'd once shared.

    I love you still...

You tell me here in this fragile present, unclouded by napalm dreams of death and atrocity, outside the phrenic pictures that still haunt your nights and worry your days, it was the thought of me alone gave you succor.

How can I do anything now but weep, for the comfort I never gave? Never there to sooth your brow, of pestilence and hate or the wails of dying comrades as you waited in that long corridor of despair.

So wide the river of time between us, its slow meander has worn thin the banks of my belief. Nearly had I forgotten, until this moment, the alchemy of your glance, how your smile curves like the arc of a hawk's wing in flight, carrying me with you beyond sorrow's realm.

My love,

Today the war has claimed us both,
with creeping tendrils it has climbed the wall of decades since, to breach the ramparts of denial and splinter the mortar of my faith.

Linda Breeden

Fallen son

In the still cool of morning, I will leave you.
I, sorrow's shadow, loosed upon the patterned hills,
mist-laden and heavy with the last dying voice of
summer's bloom.

Hard against the edge of my resolve,
my heart bridled fast, unlistening and uncaring of
weary limbs that argue harsh against my stride, I'll go.

And in the low places of fen and heather,
the linnet will winnow speckled wings and trill his songs
to coax my spirit home.

But home, home is far and lost,
a dream upon the waking,
gone with the last dying breath that you drew
as the cleft in your side bled my heart's solace.

Farewell my son, I'll not return where willow and aspen
blow, over fair England's hills to your grave in the
hollow where, eternal, you'll sleep beloved.

In every lifetime there is delight in nature...

Linda Breeden

Symbiosis

There's mistletoe growing in the laurel oak,
amid the boughs and splayed fingers of branch,
it draws provision from its host, keeping alive its own
greening against the somber winter...

and under the sea, sequined by the dance of light on
waves that crest then melt away in fluent shivers,
a remora rides the belly of a shark on its way to an
unknown rim.

Elsewhere, a meadow metropolis buzzes awake
to a flurry of wings and cicada banter, and
a cattle egret stands atop his bovine dais
plucking vermin from its hide.

Around us all, affinity reveals itself,
the intricate lacing of life upon the earth's canvas,
each form, a fragile stitch, dependent on the whole,
greater for its belonging.

Writing at the beach....

I'm trying to write
but the wind is playing with my hair,
still able to find me, even under this big umbrella
where the sun cannot.

Away from the road din and honking horns
I seek to collect my thoughts
but the far rumble of thunder and the sharp scolding
of the terns reminds me that back to nature is not
always serene.

Sandy babies with powdered-sugar bottoms exercise
their mothers and draw my attention from the page
and the tiny girl in the pink and green suit looks at me
through her legs, frowning an upside down smile.

Seagulls, stirred to a frenzy by the little boy with the
crackers, object to being ignored even if you don't
have crackers.
Their black heads cropped like executioner's hoods,
they sneer at me as if I were a wedding guest with no
gift.

And the sandpiper at the water's edge must have a
new pair of shoes he's afraid to get wet as he runs
back and forth with deliberate urgency
from the washing waves.

I glance to see the little girl in the bathing suit up to
her waist in sand.
Her mother's buried her and now runs to the water's

Linda Breeden

edge to coax the baby from her sandy shell.

The child pops out one leg – amazed it's still there,
then the other, and runs to her parent.
I wonder how I'll ever get anything written as, a short
while later, she tries to bury her mother in sand – towel
and all.

Again, I work to focus my thoughts but the sails in the
distance and the bodies dangling like spiders from
invisible threads of parasails cause my mind to wander
outward to the sea and the lure of unsure footing.

Pretty soon I'll have to get up and walk down the
beach where the shells and the sea wash will again pull
my attention -- downward this time.
Enough of this beach chair and sitting!
I guess the only writing I'm going to get done is this
poem.

Caterpillar Spring...

Long I gazed on morning skies, like cirrus fields of cotton, remembering dreamy days of youth, so many years forgotten.

How real they seemed, those moments passed, so vivid then before me. Such stretch of time was spanned just then and youth so implored me.

Lazing in the fields just wakened to warbler's tireless trill, I saw abound through tender eyes such life that stirs me still.

Over the ground in random throng, in yellow-petaled mane, in reborn glory graced by spring, the dandelion did reign.

Here and there in scattered cliques with boughs of silver hue, poplars swayed in spring tide's breath -- Aurora's twinkling dew.

And in the thicket edging near through scouts of wild rose, the caterpillar soon would wake from winter's webbed repose.

I couldn't wait to wake them up, those sleeping fuzzy knaves, and watch them inch from leaf to leaf like little wooly waves.

It mattered not to one so young that they would soon conspire to strip their host with greedy jaws of all it's green attire.

Linda Breeden

What cared I, with all my life so new, of serious things,
I only saw those leafy leavings sculpt like lacy wings.

But now the day calls me back and gently so
persuades, that all the magic we perceive is magic we
have made.

No different are the days of youth than seasons still
remembered yet only innocence can see life's beauty
humbly tendered.

I now see through wakened eyes how time and age
have fooled me, how disappointment's bitter taste
and touch have sternly schooled me.

How into life had entered doubt of springtime's
certain waking and with the days and years that
passed my life I'd been forsaking.

But somehow, like a gentle breeze blown softly 'cross
the years, the truth of youth and simple joys will
vanquish all my fears

Now I see with reborn heart how sweet my soul can
sing, and now my heart anticipates a caterpillar spring.

In every lifetime there are ordinary pleasures...

Linda Breeden

The front porch swing

It was really a glider;
I just called it the swing on the front porch.
Long as a sofa and tufted, with a ruffled skirt and
wrought iron runners, it gently creaked a squeaky
chorus to the rhythm of my sway.

I'd lie in it during those languid
days of childhood, sprung from school by summer
break, gently rocking in the sultry mornings.
Around me birds flitted like feathered stars
in a firmament of green, coaxing me beyond my perch.

Some of my greatest adventures were
launched from that swing, a book above my head,
catching moonbeams with Peter and Tink.
Laying aside my pact with gravity, unhindered by
disbelief, I'd fly beyond the humdrum world,
my body safely ensconced in that front porch swing.

Nurse

She comes when I am sleeping.

On the highway, I walk the dark divide between
oblivion and flight, my thoughts struggling to discern
reality's edge.

From down the hall I hear laughter,
or is it far away, wafting from a lone cottage
silhouetted against the shore by night's drowsy brow?

She speaks my name.

I feel myself return, carried back on morphine winds,
through sterile corridors, to this room.

"How are you feeling?" she asks,
her voice a pardon from the pain's indictment.

I smile in answer as
butterfly hands flutter around me,
winging my thoughts to a safer shore.

Linda Breeden

The barn

Under an ordinary corner of sky, on land
sliced perfect as a ship's prow from the
lower forty of McCaully's farm, it stands.

Martyred by interstate proximity,
eroded by the foul breath of ten thousand passing
cars spewing their noxious rebuffs of bucolic life, it
endures.

Derelict under the angry sun of forsaken days,
once rich with purpose and simple means, its only
company now, a sorrel mare, content to graze on the
harsh fodder of irrelevance.

In the heart of Ohio's farmland, abandoned
at the edge of nostalgia's farthest border,
lamenting quietly the days long past, it waits.

In every lifetime there is a spirit voice...

Linda Breeden

The White Bones of Winter

This time of year,
when winter's edge bled the last colors of optimism
from the mountainside, you travelled north to
resolve the paradoxes which ruled your life.

On the dirt path
beside the water, beyond sight of the house, gazing
past crumbled walls to the stillness below, you
walked in company of your demons.

From the lake,
rising with the morning mist, the loon's lament,
harbinger of cheerless days and the
urgencies of sorrow, would feed your malaise.

Beneath your feet,
the rustle of leaves offered little reprieve
from the past's ceaseless indictment, its memories
pervading your reverie like the napalm stench of war.

You asked the trees
their understanding, asked the day forgiveness for
what could not be spoken when the heart is laid raw
and answerable for the sins of its own hands.

Came the answer;
weep not for the fallen, for the dead walk unfettered
through all the seasons of man, but regrets, the
regrets of the living will bind them fast, and rattle
forever in their souls like the white bones of winter.

Spirit

You are the river,
not the miry bank or jagged rock
that divides the torrent's rush.

You flow through lifetimes in supple flesh,
wearing bodies smooth as river stones,
as you wend your way through arteries of silt and
dreams.

Issue life into the motley beasts but claim no lineage
to claw and bone.
They are but your fancy, not your forebears,
and decision your only antecedent.

You are the wind,
not the schooner's sail,
that slack awaits, its canvas lung,
the inhale and exhale of the sky.

You blow the tempest of human passion
'cross a pale and anguished plain,
and excite men's minds to madness
just to have a game.

This world before you scatters
like the grains of a mandala,
Its shards of lifetimes rearranged by your ever-
changing whim, as you breathe softly back the breath
of life into the eternal circle.

Linda Breeden

You are the sun, not the spinning earth
that, frigid, shivers in heaven's black expanse.
Yours' the preternatural flame,
that shines through corridors of earthly guile,
illuminating the self forgotten by this lost and
temporal world.

It is you, unseen star, that ignites the spark of
sentience, you, clear shadow, who animates the
lissome willow and cajoles the fragile grass to clamber
in the fields toward your warmth.

Feel the cadence of eternity beyond your own
heart's beating.
Shine forward the light of truth into the unborn days.
Life's ascendant claim is yours to this world of
unbelievers.

Sleep Walker

Another night,
this time I wake to hear your footsteps on the floor
above. My little one you're walking through your
dreams again, worrying the rugs and the darkness...
and me.

What urgency invokes your restless feet to wander,
searching for something unseen in these opaque
hours, beyond the purview of dreams, beyond the
comfort of this house?

Each night the same, in stealth you flee your bed,
eyes hollowed out by the unrequited closure of
a curse none have witnessed outside your shadow
world.

Last night, again, the squad car at our door,
down by the tracks they found you,
this time, waiting by the train, a small specter haunting
the crossing near the water tower.

What, my child, could fret one so young,
churn your world with such desperate burden,
that you hunt the night in search of peace,
like tide pulled fast by the moon.

Still, you never remember when you wake.
You blink at the world through tearful eyes,
the window of insight shut once more from within,
this weary guardian turned away

Linda Breeden

Tonight I follow, downstairs through the hall,
trailing your frame like a vanishing sprite,
through the screen to the darkness outside,
where I catch you before you fly.

I hold you, but don't wake you from your private
umbral world, the inky morn thrusts starlight spears
through the dogwood copse, ghost white on the hill,
slouching steeply down from the porch.

"Why do you cry," I whisper to you across that
troubled chasm, as I watch you coax your memories to
words, plumbing the depths of unfathomed grief,
to purge your soul of pain.

In the hush before cockcrow comes my answer,
in trembling confession to the listening night, your
swollen eyes glistening with sorrow, your child's voice
raw with despair as you lay down your terrible burden.

"I didn't mean to do it," you begin so slowly,
"I just couldn't brake," comes the threnody of sobs.
(I reach for your hand to comfort your telling,)
"I didn't mean to kill the child."
....

So silent the morn in benediction.
Your breathless words now belong to this night.
Are they demons your young soul has summoned,
or a past life more real than dreams?

Come closer my son, rest your head in my lap.
We'll listen to trees whisper low with the night wind,
as the strains of yesterday snake from your mind
to leave you at last in peace.

Because

Because men worship beauty, we disdain ourselves
if we are not beautiful, cursing every unsmooth
surface of our form.

Because men admire opulence we chide ourselves
if we have not, coveting our brother's fortune in the
sting of paucity.

Because there are those who say only the meek will
triumph, we lessen ourselves, finding glory in frailty or
defeat, and sin in abundance.

Because doctors have said we are just physical, our
thoughts and emotions the sum only of brain
reactions, we believe we cannot find our way back
from unhappiness alone.

Because the world is a serious place, full
consequence and greed, we separate ourselves,
not realizing the world is ours to change.

Because bodies grow old and all life forms wither,
we assume we will die, forgetting we are not of this
world but merely in it.

Because this material plain of force and hunger
persuades us that man cannot win,
we deny our ascendancy and ourselves
and forget our choice in this game.

Linda Breeden

Joy

Have you ever toiled, spent and weary, just for the delight, for that hard-won struggle of flesh and spirit against surly nature?

Have you felt your fists clenched strong and your back stiffened in resolve and known no force from gods or men could move you?

And in the quiet time when Earth yawns at sleepy dusk and the evening sky slinks chameleon-like across the heavens, changing mood and form, do you ever touch that distant point, that far horizon of fading azure and know that you are there?

Has your pulse raced to cut the wave with towering mast and sail, as you thrilled for the glimpse of that distant shore seductive as tomorrow?

Have you dreamt, have you beheld, have you embraced the wonder of your fellow man in his struggle to be free, and wept the tyrant's cruelty?

Have you heard the riot of song stir within, when you've given your heart away, and felt the longing for an untamed passion, course the pathways of your blood?

Then my friend you have known joy, a joy no mere flesh could conceive, for you are the maker, the dreamer, the dreamed, eternal; the soul of man.

In every lifetime there is awe and the spark of wonder...

Linda Breeden

La Giaconda

In your company, jealousies writhe unformed on the lips of strangers.
Set against a pale world, lessened in hue by the loveliness of your gaze, all comparisons cease, save the nuanced breath of awe.

A supernal bow draws ethereal chords from out the hollow body of heaven, trembling vibrato pleas for the favor of your smile. Its voice, a dulcet yearning, falls lightly upon the world.

Though not flesh and sentience, still you coax the faith from mortal swains, capturing with your aspect the copious dreams of Eden in only a single glance.

Smile Mona, across the ages... you winsome painted coquette.

Outlanders

Before daybreak, I hear the wet air
buzz in the high-tension wires above
as I walk below these towers of sagging strands,
which run like scalloped nerves across the land.

From here the stanchions puncture the sky,
gaunt metal girders braced against the Earth,
rising and narrowing to cross supports which cinch
their resolve like steel Atlases,
shouldering the burden of the world's potential.

I wonder at their end, at the rush of electrons
racing through corridors to distant destinations,
eager to light the mornings of the waking
who, with a flip of a switch or push of a button,
will direct them to their tasks.

Through fragile filaments, an onslaught of
outlanders streams into our homes,
Trojan particles charging unseen on wire wings
to animate waiting soldiers.

What is this force that surrounds us, loops above,
flows through hidden, with the power to change our world,
light our paths

... eavesdrop on our private lives?

Linda Breeden

The pied piper

The girl has an edge -
not the sharp cutting edge of a caustic wit,
or the dull hardened edge of a street-wise high
priestess wary of too many ambitious disciples.

No, hers is an edge more ragged and rhythmic,
like back alley jazz, beatnik and bohemian,
uncomplicated, yet coolly disquieting.

She leads with that edge like a sounding clarion,
an unwitting pied piper, unapprised of the
consequence of her air.

Atlantis

Come, my love, to the wind-tower, high above the world; we'll gaze for one last time upon our fair Atlantis, crucible of justice and liberty that, for this brief breath in eternity, outshines the stars.

Come, while the night is ours and the mirror sea still reflects the universe's aeonian promise, while clouds yet hold their tears and whisper soft goodbyes to this, the last shining refuge of free men.

Come, please come, for time grows short and Atlantis so soon a memory. My heart, it aches for her silvered grasslands and the providence of her woods, hoary and mystic, politic and wise as the soul of her fated race.

Come feel the caress of the night-wind as it splays your hair like a lover's fingers, and beckons you home to the waiting stars that long for your return, and gently promise the hope of forever past the ruin of this night.

Come float among the spires, alabaster white, glistening in the moonlight. You, in robes of aubergine, with ivory skin and willow eyes, resplendent in the night's embrace, shall remain my purest thought.

Hold me now we'll face this cruel night as we watch our death approaching, I glimpse
the fire in the distant sky as it hurls its way toward our doom and I know we'll not see the sun rise again o'er

Linda Breeden

the ianthene eyes of morn.
Come, my love, to the wind-tower, high above the
world, we'll gaze for one last time upon our fair
Atlantis, crucible of justice and liberty that, for this
brief breath in eternity, outshines the stars.

Majillon

Before the celestial paradigm, before the pull of gravity culled the fragments of the world together, when life was yet formless and unfettered by eyes or legs, wings or breath, there arose those beings, custodians of wisdom, who could foretell the path of life as it turned to a joining with the universe,

Spirits who would remain without form, apart from the game, whose counsel, it was said, could conquer the blackest heart and vindicate even the callous void of death.

Such was the legend of the oracle of Caldor, numen of the Mithrial wood.
...
In the ancient days of Majilon
when summer wore her skirts embroidered
with the colors of the meadow,
and the enchanted songs of faeries
rose up from the weald to beguile the rough beasts
lazing in their fields, he set out for the low hills
far beyond the hearth of home.

His lord's amulet he carried in a pouch at his side,
the ring of fair Elamere pressed close to his heart,
the fire of resolve in his eyes.
Said his liege, "Go you, Braewyn, to the place in the hills, from where shines the light of knowledge, my daughter feels the hand of the dark lord Death and you her only hope."

Linda Breeden

Laurel eyes and raven hair, Elamere, warm as
sunlight, had captured his heart with her gentle gaze
and unyielding strength of will, that endured the whims
of capricious fortune and her destiny of sorrow.
Hard he'd fallen before her heart, a helpless captive
swain, who held her higher in his regard than all that
world's esteem.

So journeyed Braewyn to the hills of Caldor,
with falcon eyes and a sorcerer's cunning,
his bow and quiver at the ready,
his blade slung close in its sheath.
He carried the days into the nights to find that
primordial light, for the life of his dying Elamere,
his one and true beloved.

.....

Into the magic lands he went
where willows slouched toward marshy dales,
and listened with leafy ears
to discern the machinations of the creatures
that crawled and scurried and slithered there
in that strange enchanted place,
where even the wind was wary.

No path to lead him, no sign to guide,
for the land reformed like swells on the sea,
sloughing its skin of rock and mire,
a terra serpent wriggling to ether,
a trembling mirage in a desert deception,
twisting and shimmering 'til his step was unsure,
it covered his trace with each step he trod.

A lone hawk, on the second morn,

Through the canopy

lazing in circles high above,
cried out from its slant beyond the hills,
a winged portent imbibing the fear of those who
would seek the truth.
But none there were who had heard that telling,
for consumed by fears that ruled their hearts,
all bled their failures on altars of shame
to never be heard again.

Three wearying days Braewyn ranged the low hills,
dour and bleak as his heart,
that world's twin suns, his only guides, watched with
callous regard.
But on the last of those desolate days,
beyond, in the low hanging sky,
through saffron clouds, he glimpsed floating there,
a castle of polished stone,
which hung o'er the Mithrial wood.

Across its vast enchanted realm
feathered leviathans swooped and climbed,
their snowy wings catching the light
as it played in the morning sky.
A nascent belief began to rise
as he watched from his earthbound station,
and wonder soon found him, coaxing him skyward
from the land that held him fast.

Siren songs on the languid breeze
sifted down from that magical place,
and bade him stop to relinquish his aim
as he felt his body pulled skyward.
So strong was their urging he feared his resolve
would part like the drifting clouds
and will might crumble in the clench of their hold,

Linda Breeden

turning too swiftly to dust.

But into his eye there crept a vision,
in graceful robes of aubergine hue,
a crown of verbena round her head, his lovely
Elamere.

She reached out her hand to lead him back
where the soft light of dawn was rising,
to the place they'd first met at the crest of the fall
where heart and soul were well claimed.

Her gentle countenance held him fast
as the ache in his heart began to swell,
the only thought could save him there
was the hope to touch her again
and feel the warmth of her giving soul,
alive and real in his arms.
So, at the sky he shouted her name,
as incantation against its urging,
and siren voices were stilled.

Quickly he strode from out of that place
into the murky weald where terror would
find him in darkness of mind
as the light from above lost its way.
He knew no direction, save the tug of his heart,
giving compass to each step he trod
as he girded his nerve to face the peril
that lurked in the thicket beyond.

Across divides of torpid streams,
black as stygian night, winding furtive through the
hoary wood, he warily made his way,
though brambled copse and scabrous cliff

Through the canopy

conspired to slacken his pace
and bark-skinned giants with gnarled limbs
creaked warning from the shadows.

Adumbral forms prowled his wake,
stealthy and undefined, their sallow eyes the color of
pain as they stalked their wary prey.
Three times his arrows met their mark
and demon beasts fell silent.
Twice his dagger slashed hungry throats
that sprung to slay their quarry, for
guile was his in the fold of night
and purpose his sharpest blade.

Limbs fagged by ordeal,
thoughts heavy with the days
that weighed on his dying Elamere,
he summoned the mettle to drive himself onward
with strength of unyielding will,
'til out of that forest of dreadful dreams,
which scourged his flesh and sullied his hope,
he came on a clearing of lambent light
that shone from a stagnant pool.

Great tufts of moss hung down from its rim,
their fringed grey drifts in the turquoise basin,
plumbed the depths of crystal water, still before its
waking.
From that pool's ensorcelled deep there rose a light
of misty mien that filled the clearing with a rapturous
peace and promise of things untold.

He knelt to touch its mirrored surface,
gaze into the watery chasm,
but saw no reflection of his own harrowed visage

Linda Breeden

between that pool and night.
Startled, he turned to the clearing's edge
casting his sight on a motionless form,
whose face lay pale and limbs
sprawled lifeless
across the threshold of that glade.

Bright points of light,
their bumble bee voices, chattering around the fallen,
darted and flickered their fragile beams in a tender
flurry of stars.
Then, to his surprise, a deliberate turning
as water now meant to speak,
and out of its bowels was heard a message
spoken voiceless to the sky.

"Welcome traveler, you who are worthy to enter upon
this glen, what truth do you seek from your perilous
journey which lies beyond your reach?"
Up spoke Braewyn to the swirling presence,
his own voice a silent asking. "How save I the life of
my dying beloved, the reason I've journeyed so far?"

From out of the hollow a laughter flowed,
encircling the space all around,
its clear vibrato of tremulous strains playing lightly on
the air.
"Look again," said the voice from the water,
"for truth lies there behind you,
the sham of death, a counterfeit end
there in your own broken form
as you watch from this place of light."

Braewyn looked on the lifeless form,
to see the face of his own ravaged self,

Through the canopy

a fragile reed cut down by the scythe,
far from the fields of home.
"Regard," said the numen, "from where you flew
and know that you are free,
for life is more than struggling sinew and narrow days
of seasons, and love casts its gaze in a widening ring
beyond the rim of life."

Then he watched as from out of that pool
a mist began to form,
in the starlit hold of night's enchantment
a gossamer figure took shape
and from her hands of limpid beams and face of
radiant vapor
there shone a promise, and joy was his
in the brilliant light of knowledge,
in the perfect truth of her being.
...

In the ancient days of Majilon,
when autumn wore its coat embroidered with the
colors of the meadow, and the enchanted songs of
faeries rose up from the weald to beguile the rough
beasts lazing in their fields, they set out from the low
hills, far from the hearth of home,
twin souls, resolute in their being,
forever free, beyond the dark rim of death.

Linda Breeden

On the star road...

She met him on the star road,
at the edge of reality and longing,
where dreams fell upward into promises and
shadow-pillars upheld the weightlessness of
becoming.

Cloaked in daffodils and yearning she
spread herself out on quivering wings
to the whispered winds of hope and
rode the updraft through the inky night on
her way to morning's insight.

But when he finally caught up with her
she was tacking hard into swells of sedition
her thoughts thunderstorms
her voice a clarion sword
thrusting up from seas of despair

She looked at him through squalls,
nations crumbling, suns exploding,
her love sent too far past to save her sight.

But he was not of time nor in it and
gathered her ages up from their abandoned
tenements on threads as thin as thought and
offered her judgment, free of sorrow outside her
nimbus eyes.

She touched his hand, his
alchemy rising to a universe of faith, and
spread herself out into the light on the cliffs beyond

Through the canopy

eternal.

He smiled a waterfall, his prism eyes shining
above her arid skies, and rained down his love a
furious torrent, to quench her thirsty soul.

And from their love, a mighty river
through a universe of pain, carved canyons of prayer
to extol forever the hope of life's divine promise .

Linda Breeden

ABOUT THE AUTHOR

Linda Breeden lives in Safety Harbor Florida with her other half (actually more like other 5/8ths , as he's quite a bit taller) and their 2 cats. An import from the New York, New Jersey area she is happy to tell friends still up north that, while it's dumping a foot of snow in their driveways, she won't be shoveling anything this winter, but she may be writing a poem about it!

By the way, if you just turned to this back page to decide whether or not you want to buy this book, the poems are much better than this biography, really!

www.ingramcontent.com/pod-product-compliance
Lightning Source LLC
Chambersburg PA
CBHW071724040426
42446CB00011B/2201